1100　1200　1300　1400　1500　1600　1700　1800　1900　2000

CANADA THROUGH TIME
First Nations
and Early Explorers

Kathleen Corrigan

capstone

Read Me is published by Heinemann Raintree,
an imprint of Capstone Press,
1710 Roe Crest Drive, North Mankato, Minnesota 56003

Copyright © 2016 Heinemann-Raintree
an imprint of Capstone Global Library, LLC
Chicago, Illinois

To contact Capstone please visit www.mycapstone.com

Edited by James Benefield
Designed by Philippa Jenkins
Original illustrations © Capstone Global Library Ltd 2016
Picture research by Kelly Garvin
Production by Victoria Fitzgerald
Originated by Capstone Global Library Limited
Printed and bound in China

ISBN 978 1 410 98119 6 (hardback)
19 18 17 16 15
10 9 8 7 6 5 4 3 2 1

ISBN 978 1 410 98124 0 (paperback)
19 18 17 16 15
10 9 8 7 6 5 4 3 2 1

ISBN 978 1 410 98129 5 (ebook)

Acknowledgments

Photo credits: Alamy/Accent Alaska.com, 26; Capstone Press/Karon Dubke, 28, 29; Getty Images: Stock Montage, cover (left); Granger, NYC, 5, 17, 18; Library and Archives Canada: Cowie, William G, PA-147444, 23, Frances Anne Hopkins, acc no. 1989-401-2, c002774, 16, Humphrey Lloyd Hime, acc no. 1936-273, c016447, cover (right), R-231-2236-6-E, 9; North Wind Picture Archives: 4, 6, 8, 10, 14, 19, 20, 24, 25, Nativestock, 7; Science Source/CCI Archives, 13; Shutterstock: Keith Levit, 22, Krasowit, 12, nfsphoto, 21, Thomas Brain, 15, ValeStock, 27; Wikimedia/D. Gordon E. Robertson, 11.

Every effort has been made to contact copyright holders of any material reproduced in this book. Any omissions will be rectified in subsequent printings if notice is given to the publisher.

All the Internet addresses (URLs) given in this book were valid at the time of going to press. However, due to the dynamic nature of the Internet, some addresses may have changed, or sites may have changed or ceased to exist since publication. While the author and publisher regret any inconvenience this may cause readers, no responsibility for any such changes can be accepted by either the author or the publisher.

Some words are shown in bold, **like this**. You can find out what they mean by looking in the glossary.

Contents

The first explorers

Explorers travel to new places. Some travel to places no one has seen. Other explorers visit places that are new just to them. The first people to explore and settle in Canada were **ancestors** of the **Aboriginal** people. We think they came between 10,000 and 40,000 years ago! English and French explorers did not visit Canada until the 1500s.

There were already many groups of **First Nations** people and **Inuit** in Canada when explorers from Europe came to visit and settle.

Aboriginal life

Aboriginal people had different ways of taking care of themselves. For example, they all made clothing that kept them warm. Some eastern **First Nations** people hunted animals and fished. Others planted the "three sisters"—corn, beans, and squash.

First Nations people made canoes using things around them, such as wood.

DID YOU KNOW?

Some Aboriginal groups created new ways to travel, such as with kayaks and snowshoes. They also drummed, sang, and danced.

The Plains **First Nations** people hunted bison. They ate the bison and used them to make clothing and tools. They created tent-like shelters called tipis from bison hides. These groups moved from place to place to follow bison herds.

The West Coast First Nations people made tools out of wood, stone, and shells. They hunted, fished, and found plants to eat.

Plains tipis were made out of bison hide wrapped around tall poles.

The West Coast First Nations people used wood to make houses and canoes.

The Vikings

Viking explorers came to Canada around AD 1000. The Viking Leif Ericsson and his crew sailed from Greenland to Newfoundland. They met the Beothuk **First Nations** people who lived there.

The Vikings only stayed for a few years. No one knows for sure why they left. After they were gone, no Europeans came to North America for almost 500 years.

L'Anse aux Meadows in Newfoundland was the first European **settlement** in North America.

Europeans begin to explore

The next explorers arrived in 1497.
John Cabot and his crew sailed from
England. They arrived on the coast of
Newfoundland. Jacques Cartier arrived
in 1534 to find gold. Cartier met
First Nations people. He claimed their
land for France.

John Cabot found
the oceans were full
of codfish.

Jacques Cartier showed First Nations people beliefs that were popular in Europe.

13

Europeans begin to settle

In 1604 the explorer Samuel de Champlain arrived from France to explore Canada. He brought French **settlers** who wanted to stay. Their first **settlement** was Port-Royal in Nova Scotia. The settlers began to trade with **First Nations** people who lived there. The Europeans traded things such as axes, knives, and pots to get beaver furs.

The early settlers lived together surrounded by log walls.

Beaver furs were used to make hats and beaver coats. They became popular in Europe.

The Voyageurs

The Voyageurs explored Canada by canoe. They were men who carried furs and other goods through the **wilderness** to trade. Voyageurs also sent furs back to Europe. **Aboriginal** guides helped the Voyageurs go further and further west.

Aboriginal guides helped Voyageurs go further west than they had gone before.

DID YOU KNOW?

Some explorers and Voyageurs were very young. Étienne Brûlé was 16 when he was sent to live with the **First Nation** Wendat people. Over time he learnt their languages and customs. He also explored four of North America's Great Lakes with the Wendat.

C.W. JEFFERYS

Settlers in the 1800s

Settlers built many forts in the 1800s. A **fort** protected settlers from attacks by other Europeans, Americans, or **First Nations** people. The new settlers wanted to own, build, and grow food on the land. They got their wish, but pushed the **Aboriginal** people away.

Missionaries from Europe came to Canada.

DID YOU KNOW?

Forts isolated settlers
from First Nations people.

The Inuit

Some Europeans sailed north of Canada. They met the **Inuit** people who lived in the Arctic. Europeans brought guns, cloth, metal, and tools to trade with Inuit people. Inuit people helped Europeans survive the cold weather. For example, they built igloos.

The Inuit also showed Europeans how to use animal parts to make warm shelters (or tents), coats, and waterproof shirts.

DID YOU KNOW?

The Inuit built stone landmarks called Inukshuk. Inukshuk told the Inuit of safe ways to travel across the land. Others were made to remember a special person.

The Métis

Europeans travelled far across Canada to explore, trade, or work. Some Europeans married **First Nations** women. The wives helped the traders to survive—they knew how to work on the land. The children of the **settlers** who married First Nations people were called the **Métis**.

The Métis language, Michif, mixes French, English, and **Aboriginal** languages.

Métis built their own **settlements**.

Western Canada

Many Europeans visiting Canada's west coast did not settle there. In the 1790s and 1800s, Sir Alexander Mackenzie and Simon Fraser helped to change this. **First Nations** people and Voyageurs helped them find rivers. Furs could be carried down rivers to the Pacific Ocean. Soon, new **settlers** built **forts** to protect this trade.

Some **Aboriginal** people welcomed Sir Alexander Mackenzie and Simon Fraser (right). Others put up a fight.

DID YOU KNOW?
Totem poles were made to help people remember stories, families, and special people.

Many nations

There were many **Aboriginal** nations in Canada before Europeans arrived. Each group had its own culture and traditions, from dances to prayers. These showed respect for nature and the Earth.

Today, Canada has people from all parts of the world. It is still a country made from many nations.

More than 60 Aboriginal languages are still spoken in Canada today.

People from many nations are part of Canada today.

DID YOU KNOW?

One traditional belief says that North America formed on the back of a turtle. The Aborginal name for it is Turtle Island.

Making a totem pole

Totem poles are carved from big trees. The carvings tell a story or describe a family or person. You can make a small totem pole too.

What you need:

- paper
- markers or crayons
- glue
- scissors
- paper towel roll

What to do:

1. Think of an animal for each person in your family. What animal are you like?

2. Draw and colour the head of each animal on the paper.

3. Cut out the heads. Where will you put them on your totem pole?

4. Glue the heads, facing outward, to the paper towel roll.

5. You might add wings and ears to your totem pole if you have a bird picture.

6. Show your family your totem pole. Explain what each animal or person on it means to you.

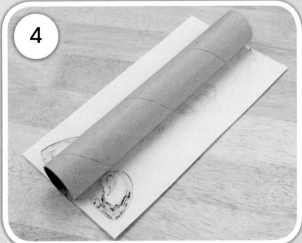

Glossary

Aboriginal original and ancestors of the people who live in a land; in Canada, this includes the Inuit and the Métis people

ancestor member of a family who lived long ago

First Nations people who have lived in Canada for thousands of years; not Inuit or Métis

fort group of strong, guarded buildings where soldiers live

Inuit Aboriginal people who live in northern Canada

Métis people whose ancestors were both European and First Nation or Inuit

missionary person on a special quest to spread word of his or her religion

settlement place where a number of people gather and build their homes

settlers people who settle in an area and build a settlement

wilderness wild area of land with few settlers

Vikings Scandinavian warriors who explored many places about 1000 years ago

Find out more

Books

The Metis: A Visual History, Sherry Farrel Racette (Gabriel Dumont Institute, 2010)

The Kids Book of Aboriginal People in Canada, Diane Silvey (Kids Can Press, 2012)

Websites

FactHound offers a safe, fun way to find Internet sites related to this book. All of the sites on FactHound have been researched by our staff.

Here's all you do:

Visit www.facthound.com
Type in this code: 9781410981196

Index